QUOTE
Me On That

Darryl Turner

Halo ●●●●
Publishing International

ISBN: 978-1-61244-301-0
LCCN: 2014945903

Printed in the United States of America

Published by Halo Publishing International
1100 NW Loop 410
Suite 700 - 176
San Antonio, Texas 78213
Houston, Texas 77205
Toll Free 1-877-705-9647
Website: www.halopublishing.com
E-mail: contact@halopublishing.com

1
January

Are you addicted to motivation? Work hard to get addicted to motivating "action" instead. Inspiration without perspiration is futile!

2
January

While many set **New Year's** resolutions, consider setting **new day** resolutions. Realize that each day is a new chance to start over.

3
January

Two types of people: **Campers** and **Climbers.**
Isn't it time to trade your tent for some
ropes?

4
January

Question: What are you using as substitutes
for **action** and **commitment**? Hint: There are
no worthy substitutes!

5
January

If you are ever wondering what to do, the answer is usually **something** as opposed to **nothing**!

6
January

Progress isn't made saying **I CAN** do it—but rather by saying **I AM** doing it!

7
January

A lack of action is only caused by either doubting the opportunity or your ability—but both can be overcome.

8
January

Success is a constant battle between **excuses** and **action**. The **excuse** or **action** we are willing to accept will completely define our future.

9
January

True faith is demonstrated only through action. If you really "believe," you WILL do your part! No action is the proof that you have no faith!

10
January

Fear makes all obstacles look bigger but action tears them down one by one!

11
January

Those with a HAND IN never seem to need a HANDOUT!

12
January

Success doesn't come from not making mistakes but learning from them. Those who fear mistakes enough to not take action have lost before they started!

13
January

Do you know the most important thing that you could do today to advance your own and someone else's life? If yes, what are you waiting for?

14
January

Getting over your problems is good! In order to get over them, it means you once were under them. Now who's on top?

15
January

The biggest cost of life is "Procrastination of the Inevitable." Take the right action today—don't delay . . . or pay the price!

16
January

Millionaire's Secret: Finish what you start and only start what matters most!

17
January

Will without skill? Fixable. Skill without will? Destined for trouble!

18
January

Mission for today: Work to turn at least one **Possibility** into a **Probability.**

19
January

Beliefs, actions, attitude, and perseverance trump any economy. Put your focus and energy on what you can control and not on what you can't!

20
January

Are you tired of hearing people say "attitude is everything?" Is it possible that you're the one they're talking about?

21
January

Elevated beliefs always lead to elevated actions ... and elevated actions always lead to elevated results.

22
January

Do you want to make today your day? The joy of the day starts with a decision to be happy. Remember: happiness is a choice, not a result.

23
January

When faced with difficult choices, we are either paralyzed or energized. Perspective is about how we choose to face our choices.

24
January

Where you are today was already determined by how you dealt with where you were yesterday.

25
January

Complaining about today is in reality criticizing your own decisions from yesterday.

26
January

Complaints are walls around your situation that lock you inside. Gratitude is the key that sets you free!

27
January

Don't complain. It is impossible to focus on your problems and leave them behind at the same time.

28
January

Denial isn't just ignoring what's wrong—it is also ignoring what's right!

29
January

Three kinds of people:
(1) Those who make a **living**,
(2) Those who make a **life**, and
(3) Those who make a **difference!**

30
January

Fear and **distraction** are the walls that stand between **possible** and **probable.**

31
January

If every day is a gift, to whom will you give your gift today?

1
February

To be able to say you're "hanging in there" means that you at least "have a grip."

2
February

No matter what yesterday brought, make the choice to be happy today: take action, and be aggressive with your goals.

3
February

Happiness is making the best of every situation instead of every situation getting the best of you!

4
February

Nobody has the ability to make you happy—
just *happier*. Being HAPPY is your job; others
can only bring the IER!

5
February

Your attitude is the first thing about you that
people notice; it resonates who you are! What
will others see in you today?

6
February

Life fact: Your attitude determines who you are to others. If they like you, it's because they like your attitude . . . and vice versa!

7
February

Life fact: Your behavior on the outside predictably will not be different from who you are on the inside.

8
February

Got influence? In other words, did you positively alter someone's life today?

9
February

The limits of your potential are bound only by the limits of your current perspective.

10
February

Happiness and generosity are contagious!
Practice them until they become you!

11
February

Show me a negative person and I will
show you someone who is unhappy
and unsuccessful!

12
February

"We will never live larger than the size of our imagination!"

13
February

Life is not about what comes at you, but about the perspective you maintain with what comes at you!

14
February

Two kinds of people: **Winners** and **Whiners.**
Whiners "blame up" while winners "game up."

15
February

There is only **progress** and **digress.** Both are a
result of how you choose to see your day.

16
February

There are two types of people: Those who see negative in the positive and those who see positive in the negative. Which one are you?

17
February

"The journey of a thousand miles does NOT begin with one step! It begins with one thought!"

18
February

Become a pathological optimist: When you believe your own positive thoughts so much that you become crazy enough to do something about them!

19
February

Naturally positive people became that way by choice, by first doing what was unnatural.

20
February

Poverty has less to do with your money than it has to do with your mindset.

21
February

Power is found in a relentless unwillingness to quit!

22
February

The spirit with which we speak inevitably will be the spirit in which we stay!

23
February

We only **truly attempt** that which we **truly believe** we can accomplish. Attempt without belief is only going through the motions.

24
February

"Child" is one word for someone with no inhibitions and whose heart hasn't stopped believing . . . another is "Genius."

25
February

Doubt is the enemy of destiny—and proof is what doubt needs—so rise to your destiny and prove doubt wrong!

26
February

You can't keep saying the wrong words but keep hoping to get the right results! Your words create belief and belief drives how hard you try!

27
February

Belief inspires action; **entitlement** breeds laziness. Can you be honest about which one you have chosen?

28
February

Never let the fear in your mind talk you out of what you believe in your heart to be true!

1
March

We tend to be influenced the most by the beliefs of those closest to us. Are your friends **pulling you down** or are you **lifting them up**?

2
March

We will not consistently perform higher than our **expectations**—which come from **beliefs,** which come from **associations**!

3
March

My personal life lesson: "If I am going to change the world, I must first change myself!"

4
March

Spend more time building your beliefs than your skills. You won't accomplish anything believing that you can't—not even with the best skills!

5
March

You only truly attempt that which you truly believe you can accomplish. Win the battle in your mind and you will win the battle in your life.

6
March

"Do not fear those who criticize you for achievement, only fear living a life that gives them no reason!"

7
March

Watch what you say. Think about it . . . you can't talk about your problems and leave them behind at the same time.

8 March

Companies do not change; people do. And those who change the fastest win!

9 March

Sometimes the hardest **step** in prospecting is to first **step** on your brakes to **stop** there in the first place!

10
March

You can't change THE market, but you can certainly change YOUR market. Your business will never rise above your level of thinking.

11
March

Top businesses spend 70% of their energy, focus, and time implementing strategies for growth. Only 30% of their time is spent running the business.

12
March

Uncommon principle: Your value in the marketplace is determined by the size of the problems that you solve for your customers and prospects.

13
March

The quality of your customer's experience is directly determined by the quantity of positive surprises that you provide for them!

14
March

"Markets increase revenue, but strategy and sales build business. You aren't growing your business if you aren't building your customer base!"

15
March

Impressions are made through **surprise**, not **service**. Service is an expectation, not a point of differentiation!

16
March

Different is as different does. Unique business strategies create unique rewards … you can never win by copying!

17
March

"Your future always starts right now. Guard each choice and action as if your entire destiny is riding on it….because it is!"

18
March

Challenge: Call a boss from your past who seemed to be a jerk at the time because they stretched you like crazy! Tell them THANK YOU!

19
March

Challenges are the catalysts of personal growth—there is no change without challenge.

20 March

If the going is getting tough and you feel all alone, you are probably on the right path. If it were easy, you would have a lot of company!

21 March

"Nobody pays attention to the predictable. You must be different to make a difference!"

22
March

"When you are in a rut, change in any direction will take you out!"

23
March

Before you can change "THE" world, you first must change "YOUR" world. Influence: it's not just a word—it's a calling!

24 March

If you do what you've always done, you WILL NOT simply have what you've always had. The world changing without you will put you further behind!

25 March

"If your life were suddenly like the lives of your five closest friends, what would you change by the end of the day?"

26
March

At the point when we dislike where we are more than we dislike the pain it will take to change it, radical improvement begins.

27
March

Change is viewed negatively when the focus is on **from what**, and positively when placed on **to what**. Where will your change take you?

28
March

"Our only real obstacle is our natural resistance to change. When we overcome that, our opportunities become limitless!"

29
March

Once we truly change for the better, it's impossible to go all the way back to the way we were before!

30
March

The pressures of life do not create character—they merely reveal it!

31
March

Don't let circumstances control your choices, but let your choices control your circumstances.

1
April

Disbelief is a learned behavior and so is the **belief** that anything is possible. The difference is which one you allow to be your teacher.

2
April

Words that are not in the Bible: Average, Halfway, Maybe, Barely, Almost, Close enough!

3
April

Find a way to bless someone today, and you
will release a catalyst of joy. Give to others
and watch your own smile increase.

4
April

Don't ever confuse **bumps** in the road with
the **end** of the road! This too shall pass! Better
times are ahead! Be encouraged!

5
April

"Train up a child in the way they should go. Lets face it, they won't know any other way!"

6
April

Do good things and someone is sure to throw rocks at you. If you catch them, you'll be ready for your next Goliath.

7
April

If you would like better connections in the world, start by connecting first with the one who created it!

8
April

Spiritual Math: Direction + Determination + Divinity = Destiny.

9
April

If we are products of our environments, then when we are unhappy with the product, we must change our environment.

10
April

Could it really be that simple? Is it possible that the only real problem you currently possess is nothing more than a lack of faith?

11
April

Building your business or your life employs a healthy balance of faith and wisdom—enough faith to take risks and enough wisdom to have boundaries.

12
April

Never forget that there were actually **two** people in the Bible who walked on water. Nothing is impossible if you step out of the boat!

13
April

Today I was told, "You can't have everything!"
My response: "Do you know who my Father
is? I already have everything!"

14
April

When we do what we fear to do, we acquire
what we previously have kept from ourselves!

15
April

"Forgive" means to give before it has been earned. A lifestyle of "forgiveness" is to consistently forgive even before you have been wronged.

16
April

His mercies are new every morning—are yours? We are forgiven as we forgive; don't expect what you're not giving!

17
April

We pray for things like patience, tolerance, and understanding. Do we realize these are the byproducts of caring, discipline, and sacrifice?

18
April

David killed Goliath, not with a rock or with a slingshot, but with pure determination! When the warrior in you rises, your giants will begin to fall!

19
April

Do not lose hope—the storm gets worse right before the breakthrough! If all hell is coming against you, then heaven is likely just ahead of you!

20
April

We tend to judge ourselves by our strengths but others by their weaknesses.

21
April

We tend to judge others not by their actions as much as by our own insecurities!

22
April

Leadership is essentially influence, so consider this: everything you say and do alters someone else's future. You *are* your brother's keeper.

23
April

If this is the day that the Lord has made, then shouldn't we also be willing to let him lead us to where he buried today's treasure?

24
April

A beating heart, the breath of life, a land of opportunity, and the love of family and God ... what more do we really need?

25
April

"You will see no shadows when facing the Son!"

26
April

Elevate others first, and you will find yourself in the process.

27
April

Isn't it amazing that whenever we manage
take our eyes off of our problems,
our blessings instantly reappear?

28
April

The Bible says, "Give **and** it will be given," not
"Give **so** it will be given." Only right motives
end up with right rewards.

29
April

When you wonder why others are running in the opposite direction, never rule out that being alone on a path often means it's the right one for you!

30
April

Have you ever considered what your life would be like if you just did all the right things that you already know you should be doing?

1
May

Seek the hand of God and you will miss His face; seek the face of God and you will find His hand.

2
May

There is only a two-letter difference between **Servant** and **Serpent**! Choose carefully **who** you are and **whose** you are!

3
May

If your aim is to lead at the top, the place to start is serving at the bottom.

4
May

Sometimes God stops you to start you; sometimes he slows you down to speed you up!

5
May

"Sometimes we find ourselves seeking things that can make us weak while avoiding the uncomfortable things that make us strong!"

6
May

We fear struggles and avoid opposition, but these are God's workout machines.

7 May

When everything seems like an uphill climb, it means that you are headed out of the valley!

8 May

If everything you see is negative then you suffer from **blessing blindness.** You need to go to the doctor and seek new **vision**!

9
May

Where there's a will there is only a **will** . . . it takes belief to make it a **way**.

10
May

Words are powerful. God made **everything** in just 6 days and never even once had to use his hands!

**11
May**

Good enough isn't good enough—unless your goal is to be average!

**12
May**

A clock shouldn't control your workday, but finishing what you were supposed to do should!

13
May

Conflict: When the thing you must do isn't the thing you want to do. Resolution: Do it anyway. Maybe Nike is right: "Just Do It!"

14
May

Courage isn't an absence of fear but advancement while fearful.

15 May

We really only have two choices in any situation: **Accept** it or **Change** it! Complaining is not a valid option.

16 May

Your challenge for today is picking the winning decision—**excuses** or **action!**

17 May

Life today is a continual compilation of yesterday's choices . . . which will continue tomorrow!

18 May

Go through, over, or around, but don't ever just stand there and look at your problems!

19 May

Whatever influences you does so only with your permission! Who or what you spend your time with is who or what comes knocking at you door.

20 May

Decisions in the PRESENT are the dividing line between the quality of your PAST and the quality of your FUTURE.

21
May

Taking the worst approach possible—to not be criticized—means only that you decided to do absolutely nothing.

22
May

Today's choices bring tomorrow's realities. In order to "realize gain" you must first "conceptualize vision" and then "energize action!"

23
May

When you hear a heard truth, you will first merely react, but soon you will have to decide whether to get better or bitter!

24
May

What you sow is what you will reap. Even weeds come from seeds. Sow cautiously—first decide what you want and then sow only those seeds.

25
May

Stress is rooted in an inability to decide, commit, and act. Likewise, it is only cured by the opposite: decide, commit, and act!

26
May

Your returns will be determined by where you choose to plant your seeds. As with real estate, planting is all about "location, location, location!"

27 May

Your life will be captured on your tombstone in the dash between the dates. Make sure you spend life dashing in the right direction!

28 May

"Nothing is more impressive or inspiring than seeing someone Giving It Their All!"

29
May

Speed is not as important as direction. What good does it do you to arrive at the wrong place quickly?

30
May

Don't ever think you will **rise** to a **low** expectation. Think **big** and **act** accordingly!

31
May

We dream BIG because there is only one other option . . . and who wants that?

1
June

Have you ever wondered how many times you didn't try something just because some-one told you that you couldn't do it?

2
June

Never strive for **normal** when **exceptional** is an option!

3
June

When a friend causes you to dream, he/she has caused you to elevate your entire life—this is a true friend, indeed!

4
June

If you can accomplish your goals without any help, then you should immediately start to set bigger goals!

5
June

Progress is a result of someone acting upon a dream.

6
June

Everything you see that is man-made started as a dream in someone's mind . . . yes, everything!

7
June

Nothing improves without the brave at heart who still dream and take risks in the name of progress.

8
June

Too many people are **Dreamers**, not **Doers**;
the smarter minority are Dreamers,
then Doers.

9
June

Success comes from experience, which comes
from failures. Inversely, failures produce
experience, which leads to success!

10
June

Don't let the possibility of failure keep you
from the possibility of success!

11
June

"Some think that being a critic makes them
look smart. It doesn't! It does, however,
point out that they lack the discipline to be
positive!"

12
June

The only way to overcome your fears is to directly engage them. First you "do it afraid," then you become "not afraid to do it."

13
June

If you let fear control you, your accomplishments will be few—but if you take courage and push past fear, it will be your limits that will be few!

14
June

We tend to criticize what we fear and we tend to fear what we don't understand—which means we criticize what we don't understand!

15
June

Success comes when we stop seeking the easy and start realizing the simple. There is nothing complicated about success; just don't fear the work!

16
June

We are constantly moving toward that on which we are focused, whether positive or negative! Make wise choices today.

17
June

Clarity must come before strategy—clarify your goals before initiating energy into action!

18
June

What we focus on tends to grow. Focus on obstacles and they get bigger. Focus on opportunities and they become more clearly evident.

19
June

Since we tend to move toward that on which we focus, we need only be concerned about where our eyes are actually aiming us!

20 June

Distraction: The loss or reduction of traction. Stay focused!

21 June

A lack of focus is not the result of the *presence* of distractions but rather the *acceptance* of them.

22
June

Great things happen when you begin to see distractions as enemies that can actually cause you to lose the battle!

23
June

You can't grasp your future while simultaneously clinging to your past.

24
June

Achievement without intention, focus, or specific actions is commonly called an accident. Win intentionally!

25
June

Learn to monitor your progress honestly. Putting more energy into the wrong plan only gets you further from where want to be that much faster!

26
June

Do you have the right focus for this week? Are you making money or making a difference? Only one of these pays lifelong dividends!

27
June

Pursuit is nothing more than predictable and intentional action that moves us closer to what we want or where we want to be.

28
June

Unless our vision is bigger than we are, it literally provides for us nothing to pursue!

29
June

Are you focused on what is actually important or surrounded by what only appears to be urgent?

30
June

The (re)birth of vision is the (re)beginning of every good possibility.

1
July

If you can worry then you can focus. They both require the same energy but are used for opposite results!

2
July

Why are some more comfortable with the certainty of their pain than the uncertainty of letting their pain go and facing freedom?

3
July

A buddy is someone who helps hide your sins while a friend is someone who will confront you . . . thus, buddies limit and friends elevate!

4
July

A true friend will risk your feelings for the sake of your future while a poser will risk your future for the sake of your feelings!

5
July

"If you plan to go places, you must expect to leave places first. What lies ahead will always require certain things to be left behind!"

6
July

Our future will be altered by every choice we make, including the ones today. Each decision brings new direction—*choose carefully!*

7
July

The future is reserved for those who will be gutsy enough to create it!

8
July

Nothing rules your tomorrows as much as the associations and influences that consume your todays.

9
July

It only takes meeting one right person to change your whole future! Keep your eyes and ears open!

10
July

How we handle the moment will determine how the future will handle us!

11
July

Holding too tightly to our past means that we will have that much less of a grip on our future!

12
July

If your eyes are on your future, then your back is to your past! That perspective is the key to progress and a happier life.

13
July

An improved perspective is **always** the cornerstone and requirement of an improved future!

14
July

Vision isn't the ability to see the future but the ability to see beyond it!

15
July

There are many with perfect sight but no vision! Be cautious, as sight can get in the way of vision. One sees conditions; one envisions opportunity.

16
July

Success is not a **goal** but a **result**! Success is what we keep for ourselves while "significance" is what we give to others! Make a difference!

17
July

Today is a good day to encourage someone and lift yourself in the process!

18
July

Today would be an excellent day to surprise someone in a positive way. Make it a goal to pay for the person in line behind you!

19
July

The rising sun represents another brand new chance to make a difference for yourself and someone else!

20
July

What you have describes where you've
been . . . but what you give determines where
you're headed!

21
July

A worthy goal for the day: Focus on uplifting
others rather than outdoing them.

22
July

If you aren't striving for excellence then you are settling for average. If you can touch the bar now, it is too low—time to raise it!

23
July

Announce your goals to your peers and friends. You are 2.5 - 7 times more likely to accomplish your goals when you commit in front of others!

24
July

A renter says, "One more month and I am gone." An owner says, "I am here for the long haul." Don't rent your goals, own them!

25
July

When everything seems to be coming at you, have you ever thought about driving on the other side of the road?

26
July

It's amazing how hard some people will work . . . to avoid having to work!

27
July

Two types of people: Those who hit the ground running and those who . . . just hit the ground!

28
July

When faced with a decision. . . yes, you should definitely go ahead and make one!

29
July

You can be on the right **track** and still be in trouble if you aren't going in the right **direction**!

30
July

My goal is to make sure that those who compliment me don't turn out to be liars!

31
July

If you could change your past you wouldn't, because you could have and you didn't!

1
August

Remember—when the poop hits the fan you can always reach down and unplug it!

2
August

We should try harder on the things that matter . . . and on the rest, not so much!

3
August

"It's always a good idea to pause for 2 to 3 seconds before answering someone's question unless, of course, the question is; "Honey, do you love me?"

4
August

We rarely remember those who **serve** us but we ALWAYS remember those who **surprise** us!

5
August

Get rid of bad influences and thoughts: Never medicate what you should amputate!

6
August

The influences others have on you are a result of your permission settings. Just like your computer—inspect, adjust, and reset as needed!

7
August

Inventory all your influences, as together they will rule your life.

8
August

Here is an interesting question: Would you rather be uninformed and happy or fully informed and miserable? Think about it.

9
August

Inspiration without perspiration still equals procrastination. Remember—**Think-Do-Live!**

10
August

Is it inspiration or perspiration that gets you ahead? My answer is . . . *YES!*

11
August

Never confuse your **common** ability to know **how** with an **uncommon** ability to learn **why**.

12
August

The man who knows **what** to do can follow a system but the one who knows **why** can create one!

13
August

"Laziness is the seed of a tree of regret!"

14
August

To encourage is to add courage; to discourage is to subtract it.

15
August

Real leaders add to others the most important element of advancement—courage!

16
August

Encouragement, to add courage, is the best gift you can give, as it is courage that causes people to take steps to reach their full potential.

17
August

"Part of the calling of leaders is to elevate the thinking of those around them!"

18
August

BE the difference for someone today. Speak life and encourage those around you—the difference for them may be life and death!

19
August

The only way to know for sure if you are a leader is by checking to see whether you have any followers!

20
August

Our responsibility as leaders is to make positive impressions on everyone we meet—impressions that impact and alter the recipients' destinies.

21
August

Business wisdom from airplanes: They don't fly because their wings are "pushed" from beneath but because they are "lifted" from above.

22
August

Leadership isn't just getting people to act—it is inspiring people to move in a direction that is ultimately good for **them**!

23
August

Companies only have two types of pain:
1) Growing Pains, and
2) Hunger Pains.
If you don't have either right now, you are headed toward one!

24
August

Your best future depends on not repeating the worst parts of your past!

25
August

When you notice the writing on the wall, don't erase it—study it!

26
August

"Its unwise to think that you learned enough from experience so that you now have less to learn from what you have yet to experience!"

27
August

Don't view them as mistakes but rather that you are creating a series of unbelievably great learning experiences for yourself!

28
August

Growth comes from starting new behaviors and stopping others.

29
August

"Imagination is the elevator of success!"

30
August

Four things we all have in common:
1) the past,
2) the present,
3) the future, and
4) the ability to make our future whatever we choose!

31
August

If you are looking for the easy path, you will probably find it ... but you will hate the outcome!

1
September

The pursuit of nothing but currency leaves nothing but a poor legacy.

2
September

They who wait for the "Perfect Time" will surely miss it, as the only way to be sure it was perfect . . . is when it's behind you.

3
September

If everything and everyone is coming against you, maybe you should try the other lane!

4
September

When we experience emotional pain, a memory is embedded that we won't want to relive—but if we avoid that pain, we avoid a valuable lesson.

5
September

Make I-C-E every day—Improve Continuously Every day!

6
September

Nothing great happens without struggle. Be diligent during the rough spots as they are the proving ground that separates champs from chumps.

7
September

Remember, life will deal you a hand that it is in direct proportion to the hand that you deal life! Nothing advances you more than taking action.

8
September

Not attempting is the ultimate failure!

9
September

Perfect balance stalls progress.

10
September

Actions are the purest representation of your authentic beliefs.

11
September

If **action** is the engine, then **belief** is the fuel.

12 September

Nothing brings change faster than initiating it.

13 September

Decision is the seed of **action,** and action is the seed of results.

14
September

Success is when the DID's outnumber the SHOULD's!

15
September

Your desire to know all the details slows down your ability to progress! Turn off the news, go to work, and make a difference!

16 September

Different Is As Different Does!

17 September

"Doing" is the best classroom; "Action" is the best teacher.

18
September

The opposite of **Can't** is not **Can** but **Done!**

19
September

We will either make a way or make an excuse!

20
September

What would you do right now if you suddenly had absolutely no fear whatsoever?

21
September

The **best** plan is simply the one you **will** follow.

22
September

Having **motivation** without **activation** is like having a Ferrari without an engine!

23
September

Opportunity awaits, but only for those who seek it. **Seek** it . . . **grab** it . . . **win** it!

24
September

Actions are fueled by intentions, but outcomes are a result of true commitment.

25
September

Don't just get **through** your problems—get **over** them. Begin to dominate them or they will dominate you!

26
September

Action turns your possibilities into your probabilities.

27
September

Your possibilities and limitations have the same thing in common—YOU decide what they are!

28
September

Procrastination is the enemy of your destination.

29
September

Definition:
Progress: (noun) the opposite of digress.

30
September

Be careful not to let your "Get READY's" or your "Get SET's" outnumber your "GO's."

1
October

Nobody ever conquered anything by simply thinking about it! Action is the key to progress.

2
October

An average action still trumps a strong word.

3
October

Admitting it is step one!

4
October

Three Facts:
1) We all want to be happy,
2) I have never met a negative happy person, and
3) Yeah, you already know, don't you!

5
October

We only truly pursue that which our
ATTITUDE allows us to authentically believe.

6
October

Choosing to be happy might take discipline but it sure beats the other option.

7
October

Positives and negatives are more than just attitudes, but the literal directions for our lives that we choose every day.

8
October

No matter which attitude you choose—positive or negative—it WILL accelerate your destiny!

9
October

Don't complain about miserable co-workers. How would you turn them around if they were a sales prospect? The principles are exactly the same.

10
October

Challenge: Go one week without
complaining about **ANYTHING**
and see what changes about your life.

11
October

"To be critical is an act of the weak, but to be
willing to understand is an act of the strong!"

12
October

Your attitude is a vehicle that will take you wherever it steers you. Is yours on the right road?

13
October

Companies never hire people. They hire attitudes.

14
October

Negativity is nothing more than fear finding its way out of your heart and into your mouth.

15
October

Goal #1: Get fired up!
Goal #2: Avoid fire extinguishers!

16
October

"As leaders, we either affect others or infect them!"

17
October

Negativity is a learned behavior! If you are negative, who was your teacher?

18
October

Negativity is the voice of insecurity.

19
October

I have never met a negative, successful person—or a stingy, happy person! Have you?

20
October

If you're not winning more than rarely, you're either not working hard enough or you have a bad plan. Even a broken clock is right twice a day!

21
October

Negative thoughts are not worthy of becoming audible.

22
October

The "First Step" is always your own!

23
October

Negativity is nothing more than a lame justi-
fication for a lame effort!

24
October

The critical difference between **winners** and **whiners** is which one chooses to see opportunity in adversity.

25
October

Negativity is the product of a lazy mind!

26
October

Battery Fact: The **positive** side gives energy while the **negative** side takes it.

27
October

Do you have the POWER today? Are you **Positive, Open, Willing, Energetic,** and **Results**-oriented? If not, go back to bed and start over!

28
October

Never let your mind talk you out of what your heart knows to be true!

29
October

You can never **get** past what you cannot **see** past. One must **believe** before one can **achieve**!

30
October

Vision is the prelude and prerequisite to accomplishment and destiny.

31
October

In business, are you *competing* or *comparing*? Outdoing the competition is *comparing*, but doing something different that surprises is *competing*.

1
November

Business Growth Formula:
Reduced **Resistance** = Increased **Efficiency** =
Increased **Revenue**.
Conclusion: *Reduce Resistance!*

2
November

There is no shortcut to the summit! Quick
riches or unearned revenue cannot be
sustained in tough times. Build your business
with hard work.

3
November

The path of least resistance always leads **downward,** to the **bottom**—it has never led **upward** or to the **top** of anything!

4
November

Our issue is thinking about THE economy more than we work on changing OUR economy! Stress comes from trying to control the uncontrollable.

5
November

Is your total strategy simply trying to outdo the competition? It's impossible—you can only outdo yourself!

6
November

The number one **hindrance** or **accelerator** of our personal growth—our **associations** and anything emotionally or mentally connected to them!

7
November

Decisions alter destiny. Every little choice changes your entire life course, even if only slightly.

8
November

To face what we fear is the key to an easier tomorrow!

9
November

"Have you not apologized because something wasn't your fault? Remember: It doesn't have to be your fault to be your problem!"

10
November

Generosity is not an act but a lifestyle!

11
November

We only get to truly keep that which we are truly willing to let go of!

12
November

Be careful not to miss too many of those "Once in a Lifetime" moments!

13
November

Money is either your harvest or your seed. How you choose to see it determines how much you actually will have.

14
November

The only place where reaping comes before sowing is in the dictionary.

15
November

Attention all unemployed: It isn't a job you seek but the opportunity to serve. Stop asking if they are hiring and start asking how you can serve!

16
November

"If it seems like everything is an uphill climb, then you're likely on the right road out of the valley to the top!"

17
November

Your best isn't your best until it's your all!

18
November

We only get an average of 4,056 Saturdays in our lifetime. What are you going to do with this one? Make a difference!

19
November

If it's destiny you seek, then it's direction you need. Aim twice; shoot once!

20
November

Hang around those who cause you to dream and flee from those who cause you to doubt!

21
November

Growth always requires your dreams to be bigger than your current reality. Make your dreams like outfits into which you will one day grow into.

22
November

Woe to the one who stifles others dreams.

23
November

We always walk toward the picture in our mind; we move closer to whatever we believe. We are influenced by those closest to us, good or bad!

24
November

Pursue your dreams before your pursuits become only dreams!

25
November

By the time you see a building it has been built 3 times. In the mind, on paper, then with bricks! If you want results, start dreaming again!

26
November

Dreams are only wild to someone else who doesn't dream!

27
November

Focus is the fuel of accomplishment.

28
November

To over-focus on your past means that you are under-focused on your future!

29
November

If you have ever wondered what's in your future, just look at your closest friends' present!

30
November

Today would be an excellent day to bless someone in a memorable way.

1
December

"Action overcomes fear; unfortunately there is nothing else!"

2
December

Today's challenge: pay for the person behind you in the Starbucks drive-through. Do you have what it takes to bless a stranger today?

3
December

What we end up having in this life is a direct result of what we are first willing to give away.

4
December

You will never "stand" a chance by simply "standing" still. Take action toward your goal. Action-less people have very skinny kids!

5
December

I have never heard a kid say, "When I grow up, I want to be Vice President of The United States!"

6
December

Most people, at least once, have talked to their microwave—they have told it to hurry up!

7
December

They say, "He who dies with the most toys wins," but I say, "He who dies with the most toys IS STILL DEAD!"

8
December

If you talk to yourself at times, try not to argue with yourself too much, as eventually one of you is going to lose!

9
December

When you find or discover your gifting, develop it more. When you realize your weakness, hire someone else to do it!

10
December

Do not be afraid of slow improvements—fear only not improving at all!

11
December

When you turn out exactly like those you spend the most time with, by all means don't blame them!

12
December

Is Larry the Cable Guy your consultant? He gives the nation the best economic and life turnaround advice ever—**Git-R-Done**

13
December

Life doesn't get better when **things** get better—life gets better when **we** get better!

14
December

"Don't fool yourself…Garbage-In, Garbage-In! Most of life's garbage never gets out!"

15
December

If **pro** is the opposite of **con**, then **progress** is the opposite of **congress**!

16
December

"When the going gets tough, the tough refocus, re-energize and swing again. Striking out is the biggest part of home run training!"

17
December

"Initiative is more than just action; it's action with a purpose. Many know what to do, but get out of the way of the person who knows why!"

18
December

Expectation is the mother of action. We only truly attempt that which we truly believe we can accomplish.

19
December

The ONLY proof of belief is ACTION!

20
December

What are you using as a substitute for action and commitment? No substitutes will suffice!

21
December

Don't let the fear of making a wrong decision keep you from making any.

22
December

Making a Difference Is As Making a Difference Does!

23
December

Every action creates a new and different direction. Where are you headed today?

24
December

Two types of people: Those who say it can't be done and those who simply get it done.

25 December

Never underestimate the power of just taking ACTION!

26 December

There are two main types of employees: **Horsepower** and **Cargo.** Remember **Cargo** is removed going up steep hills; **Horsepower** never is.

27
December

What would you attempt today if you knew beyond a doubt that you would not fail?

28
December

Things don't just happen because they're "meant to be!" "Meant to be" is only the indication that "you are meant to do it!"

29
December

Fear is an emotion but courage is a choice! The choice to take action when you really don't want to can change your life.

30
December

"Don't forsake the simple to pursue the easy. Success is simple while easy has never served anyone!"

31
December

Have a safe and happy New Year. Set lofty goals, equip yourself, and partner with those who can help!

CPSIA information can be obtained at www.ICGtesting.com
Printed in the USA
LVOW07s0618140116

470399LV00003B/3/P

9 781612 443010